SOME MAJOR EVENTS IN WORLD WAR I

THE EUROPEAN THEATER

1939 SEPTEMBER—Germany invades Poland Great Britain, France, Australia, & New Zealand declare war on Germany; Battle of the Atlantic begins. NOVEMBER—Russia invades Finland.

1940 APRIL—Germany invades Denmark & Norway. MAY—Germany invades Belgium, Luxembourg, & The Netherlands; British forces retreat to Dunkirk and escape to England. JUNE—Italy declares war on Britain & France; France surrenders to Germany. JULY—Battle of Britain begins. SEPTEMBER—Italy invades Egypt; Germany, Italy, & Japan form the Axis countries. OCTOBER—Italy invades Greece. NOVEMBER—Battle of Britain over. DECEMBER—Britain attacks Italy in North Africa.

1941 JANUARY—Allies take Tobruk. FEBRUARY—Rommel arrives at Tripoli. APRIL—Germany invades Greece & Yugoslavia. JUNE—Allies are in Syria; Germany invades Russia. JULY—Russia joins Allies. AUGUST—Germans capture Kiev. OCTOBER—Germany reaches Moscow. DECEMBER—Germans retreat from Moscow; Japan attacks Pearl Harbor; United States enters war against Axis nations.

1942 MAY—first British bomber attack on Cologne. JUNE—Germans take Tobruk. SEPTEMBER—Battle of Stalingrad begins. OCTOBER—Battle of El Alamein begins. NOVEMBER—Allies recapture Tobruk; Russians counterattack at Stalingrad.

1943 JANUARY—Allies take Tripoli. FEBRUARY—German troops at Stalingrad surrender. APRIL—revolt of Warsaw Ghetto Jews begins. MAY—German and Italian resistance in North Africa is over; their troops surrender in Tunisia; Warsaw Ghetto revolt is put down by Germany. JULY—allies invade Sicily; Mussolini put in prison. SEPTEMBER—Allies land in Italy; Italians surrender; Germans occupy Rome; Mussolini rescued by Germany. OCTOBER—Allies capture Naples; Italy declares war on Germany. NOVEMBER—Russians recapture Kiev.

1944 JANUARY—Allies land at Anzio. JUNE—Rome falls to Allies; Allies land in Normandy (D-Day). JULY—assassination attempt on Hitler fails. AUGUST—Allies land in southern France. SEPTEMBER—Brussels freed. OCTOBER—Athens liberated. DECEMBER—Battle of the Bulge.

1945 JANUARY—Russians free Warsaw. FE ARY—Dresden bombed. APRIL—Americans take sen and Buchenwald concentration car Russians free Vienna; Russians take over Be Mussolini killed; Hitler commits suicide. MAY—(many surrenders; Goering captured.

THE PACIFIC THEATER

1940 SEPTEMBER—Japan joins Axis nations (many & Italy.

1941 APRIL—Russia & Japan sign neutrality DECEMBER—Japanese launch attacks against F Harbor, Hong Kong, the Philippines, & Ma United States and Allied nations declare war on an; China declares war on Japan, Germany, & I Japan takes over Guam, Wake Island, & H Kong; Japan attacks Burma.

1942 JANUARY—Japan takes over Manila; Ja invades Dutch East Indies. FEBRUARY—Japan t over Singapore; Battle of the Java Sea. AP Japanese overrun Bataan. MAY—Japan takes M dalay; Allied forces in Philippines surrender to an; Japan takes Corregidor; Battle of the Coral JUNE—Battle of Midway; Japan occupies Aleu Islands. AUGUST—United States invades Guadalc al in the Solomon Islands.

1943 FEBRUARY—Guadalcanal taken by Marines. MARCH—Japanese begin to retrea China. APRIL—Yamamoto shot down by U.S. Force. MAY—U.S. troops take Aleutian Islands I from Japan. JUNE—Allied troops land in I Guinea. NOVEMBER—U.S. Marines invade Boug ville & Tarawa.

1944 FEBRUARY—Truk liberated. JUNE—Saipan tacked by United States. JULY—battle for G begins. OCTOBER—U.S. troops invade Philippi Battle of Leyte Gulf won by Allies.

1945 JANUARY—Luzon taken; Burma Road back. MARCH—Iwo Jima freed. APRIL—Okinawa tacked by U.S. troops; President Franklin Roose dies; Harry S. Truman becomes presid JUNE—United States takes Okinawa. GUST—atomic bomb dropped on Hiroshima; Ru declares war on Japan; atomic bomb dropped Nagasaki. SEPTEMBER—Japan surrenders.

WORLD AT WAR

Battle of
Stalingrad

WORLD AT WAR

Battle of Stalingrad

By G. C. Skipper

CHILDRENS PRESS, CHICAGO

This German soldier is lucky enough to have a warm winter camouflage uniform.

FRONTISPIECE:
Some of the buildings in Stalingrad that were wrecked by Nazi bombing raids.

PICTURE CREDITS:
NATIONAL ARCHIVES: Cover, pages 6, 8 (bottom), 9 (bottom), 10 (top), 13, 14, 15 (top left, top right), 25, 26, 30 (bottom), 33, 34 (top), 37, 38
UPI: pages 4, 9 (top), 10 (bottom), 11, 15 (bottom), 16, 17, 19, 23, 29, 30 (top), 40, 43, 44, 46
U.S. ARMY PHOTOGRAPH: pages 8 (top), 22, 34 (bottom)
LEN MEENTS (MAPS): pages 12, 20, 45

COVER:
A German soldier hangs the Nazi banner from a window of a building in the ruined city.

PROJECT EDITOR
Joan Downing

CREATIVE DIRECTOR
Margrit Fiddle

Library of Congress Cataloging in Publication Data

Skipper, G.C.
  Battle of Stalingrad.

  (His World at War)
  SUMMARY: Describes the battle of World War II in which the Russians attacked and defeated the German army holding Stalingrad against impossible odds because of senseless orders from Hitler, and which signaled to the world that the Nazis could be defeated.
  1. Stalingrad, Battle of, 1942-1943—Juvenile literature. [1. Stalingrad, Battle of, 1942-1943. 2. World War, 1939-1945—Campaigns—Russia]
I. Title. II. Series.
D764.3.S7S57   940.54'21   80-27474
ISBN 0-516-04789-2

Thousands of German and Rumanian soldiers were shivering in foxholes, bunkers, and shelters just outside Stalingrad. The savage Russian winter was even crueler than usual on this night. A blizzard was raging. And nothing could keep the icy wind from cutting into the shelters. The few soldiers brave enough to look outside could see nothing but blinding snow. It was nearly dawn. The date was November 19, 1942.

Nearly a year and a half earlier, on June 22, 1941, Nazi Germany had attacked Russia with sudden viciousness. Within three weeks, the Germans had driven far into Russia. One army group had gone as far as 450 miles. They had pushed to within 200 miles of Moscow itself.

Less than two years after the Germans and Russians signed a non-agression pact (above), Germany invaded Russia and destroyed many important Russian cities. Kiev, below, fell to the Germans even though Soviet armored units such as this one battled furiously.

The Germans left little but rubble and burned out buildings
in the Russian city of Minsk (above and below).

This German tank (above) is part of the assault force that blitzed into Russia from the Polish-Russian border on June 22, 1941. A Russian antitank gun crew (below) watches the approach of a German mechanized unit.

Above: A town in the Belgorod area that was leveled by the Nazis.
Below: A monk stands in front of an eleventh-century
Russian Orthodox monastery that was mined and blown up by the
Germans in November, 1941.

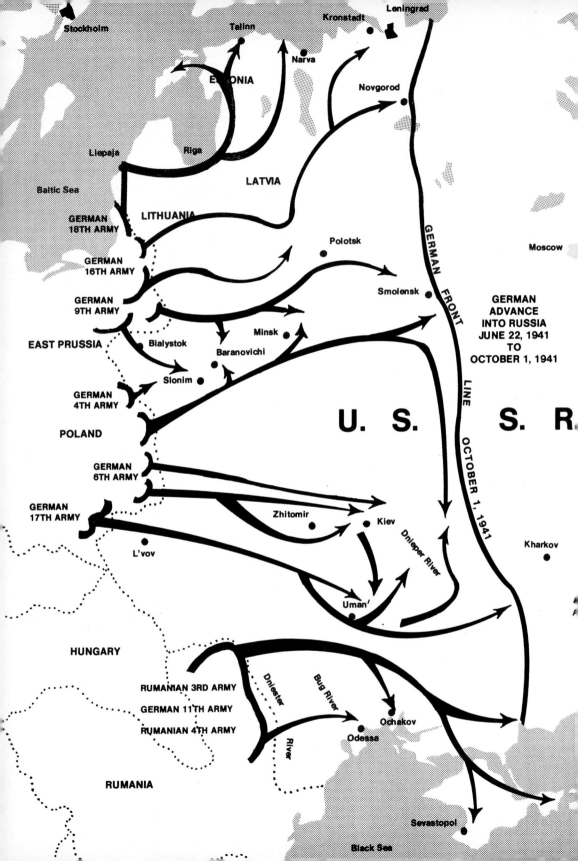

These German planes are about to bomb a bridge near Novgorod.

Before that first terrible winter had stopped them from fighting, the Germans were within 100 miles of Moscow. And they were at the very gates of Leningrad. In fact, Leningrad was almost completely surrounded by German troops. In the south, the Nazis had captured many cities, including Kiev, Odessa, and Kharkov.

During the following spring and summer, the Germans had pushed on toward Stalingrad.

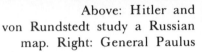
Above: Hitler and von Rundstedt study a Russian map. Right: General Paulus

German General Friedrich von Paulus was in command of the Sixth Army. Between August 4 and September 3, 1942, Paulus had taken the Sixth Army to within three miles of Stalingrad. On August 23 and 24, Nazi air attacks turned the city into a heap of rubble. By the end of September, German troops were fighting inside the city itself.

The Russians in and around Stalingrad had fought back with amazing strength. They were determined to defeat the Germans. But Germany's leader, Adolf Hitler, was sure that Russia would fall. He wanted to crush the country. He wanted to strip her of her valuable crops, industry, and minerals. And he wanted her people dead.

Adolf Hitler was not satisfied with taking Russian Cities and capturing Russian troops (above left). German troops routinely murdered Russian civilians as well. A Russian woman (above right) finds a friend or relative among those murdered by the Germans. Below: A German siege gun fires on the city of Stalingrad.

The Russians used a variety of transportation to maneuver in the snow, including tanks (above) and armored air sleds (below).

A Russian cavalry unit patrols the front in winter uniforms.

On this November night, the German and Rumanian troops outside Stalingrad were bracing themselves for another long, terrible Russian winter. When it got too cold to fight, they planned to dig in and pray that spring would come soon.

Suddenly the earth itself seemed to erupt. The howling winds of the blizzard were drowned beneath a deafening noise.

The Russians were launching a counter-attack in the middle of a blizzard! Out of the blowing whiteness, Russian soldiers and tanks appeared. They looked like phantoms.

Strange-looking tanks lumbered toward the troops outside Stalingrad. The Germans and Rumanians had never seen tanks like this before. They were the huge T-34s. Antitank guns were useless against them. The huge shells lobbed by the guns struck the T-34s and bounced off. The Russian tanks and the Russian soldiers kept coming. They did not stop.

Soon, the Russians had broken through the Rumanian Third Army line northwest of Stalingrad. They attacked the German Fourth Panzer Army and the Rumanian Fourth Army south of Stalingrad. They hit with surprise and harshness. It was only a matter of time before the south line was broken.

Inside these two lines, nearly at the city of Stalingrad, was General Paulus's German Sixth Army.

A Russian antitank gun near Stalingrad

Suddenly, the radio at Sixth Army headquarters began to crackle. The reports began
to come in. All the news was bad. The north line
had collapsed. The Russians had broken
through. They could not be stopped. The south
line was also collapsing. From all fronts there
came nothing but bad news for the Nazis.

Paulus paced up and down his headquarters.
Each report he received was worse than
the one before. Finally, he turned to an aide
and said, "We have no choice. We must move
west in a retreat. Otherwise we'll be
surrounded by the Russians. Get a message
to Hitler!"

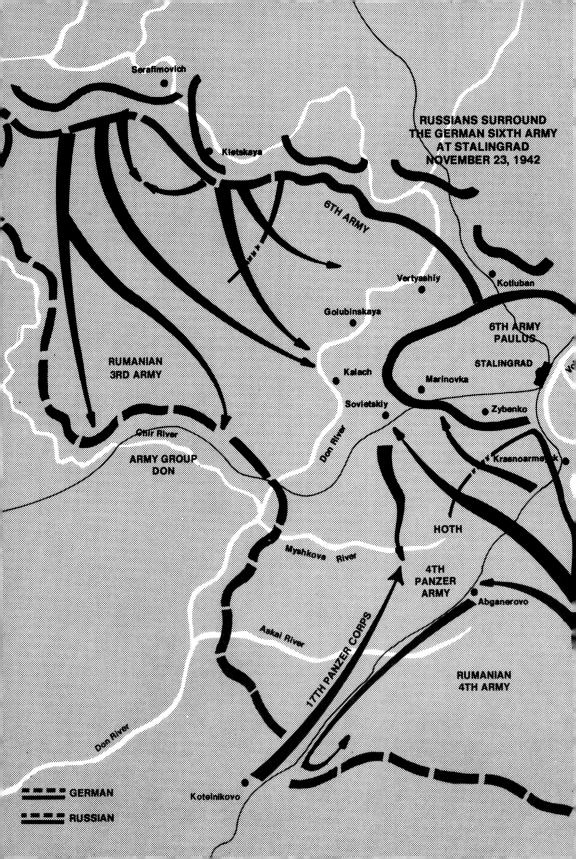

RUSSIANS SURROUND
THE GERMAN SIXTH ARMY
AT STALINGRAD
NOVEMBER 23, 1942

Serafimovich

Kletskaya

6TH ARMY

Vertyashiy

Kotluban

Golubinskaya

6TH ARMY
PAULUS

RUMANIAN
3RD ARMY

Kalach

STALINGRAD

Marinovka

Sovietskiy

Zybenko

Chir River

ARMY GROUP
DON

Don River

Krasnoarmeysk

HOTH

Myshkova   River

4TH
PANZER
ARMY

Askai River

Abganerovo

17TH PANZER CORPS

RUMANIAN
4TH ARMY

Don River

Koteinikovo

GERMAN

RUSSIAN

General Paulus's request quickly arrived at Hitler's headquarters. The German generals urged Hitler to allow Paulus to fight his way out. The Sixth Army would then be able to regroup and push back the Russians.

Adolf Hitler glared at his generals. He sat behind a desk. His close-cropped moustache twitched. His eyes narrowed to slits. Suddenly he slammed a fist down on the desk and leaped to his feet.

Shocked, the German generals watched Hitler.

"I won't leave the Volga!" Hitler screamed. "I won't go back from the Volga!"

Seething with anger, Hitler then ordered the Sixth Army to stay put.

Within four days, the Russian troops had closed in from the north and the south. They met with a loud victorious cheer at Kalach, forty miles west of Stalingrad. They had surrounded the German Sixth Army.

The German generals knew that Goering (at right with folded arms) would not be able to supply the Sixth Army with the small number of planes in his Luftwaffe.

Immediately, Paulus sent another message to Hitler to let him know the situation.

Hitler fired back an order. Paulus was to move his headquarters into Stalingrad itself. "Goering has assured me we can supply the Sixth Army by air," Hitler's message said. "The Luftwaffe can get supplies to you. You are not to retreat."

The German generals were horrified. They looked at Hermann Goering's fat, confident face and shuddered. What he had promised Hitler was impossible! To supply the Sixth Army would require 750 tons of supplies *every day*! Goering's Luftwaffe didn't even have enough airplanes to do that kind of job.

Inside the city, time dragged by. The streets had been turned into rubble by the air attacks that had continued since August 23. The city was in a state of siege. Street fighting had been going on since September. The Germans were fighting the Russians for every building and every block. The Germans fought bravely. But the Russians fought just as bravely. They hated these Nazis who had invaded their homeland.

Above: A German machine-gun post in a suburb of Stalingrad.
Right: The street fighting in Stalingrad produced destruction such as this throughout the city.

The Russian winter bore down on the Nazis. Food began to run out. Medical supplies were scarce. Ammunition was nearly gone. And the thin German uniforms gave very little protection against the bitter cold of Stalingrad. Nearly all the soldiers wrapped their thin army-issue blankets over their heads and shoulders for a little added warmth. They warmed their hands over small fires made from furniture found in ruined buildings.

And, once in a great while, they found ways to ignore the terrors of war for a short while.

One soldier wrote of stopping in amazement at seeing a grand piano in the middle of a side street. Apparently, it had been removed from a building that was about to be blown up. The soldier watched as every passing German stopped to play a few notes or a song or two. He himself was not able to play, though he had been a concert pianist before the war.

Grim German soldiers defend a makeshift post in the ruins of Stalingrad.

Frostbite had destroyed the three middle fingers of his right hand and the little finger of his left hand. And then a friend of his, who was also a pianist, sat down to play. He played Beethoven's *Appassionata* as a hundred soldiers squatted silently in the snow around him to listen. It was probably the last time any of them would hear such music.

As the winter continued, temperatures dropped lower and lower. Thousands of German soldiers starved to death, froze to death, or died of their wounds. Many of them began to go mad.

Meanwhile, the German generals pleaded with Hitler. Something had to be done. Two hundred thousand German soldiers were fighting and dying inside Stalingrad. They must be saved.

Finally, Hitler realized that the Sixth Army could not be supplied by air. He ordered General Fritz Erich von Manstein to relieve General Paulus at Stalingrad. On December 12, 1942, General Manstein launched an attack against the Russians to try to rescue the Sixth Army. The temperature was well below zero when Manstein's forces began their march.

Both Manstein and Paulus had wanted the Sixth Army to fight its way out of Stalingrad. Paulus could retreat westward to meet Manstein. They knew that would be their only hope against the strength of the Russians. But Hitler would not hear of it. He had gone into a rage at the very idea of retreating German soldiers. Again, he had ordered Paulus to stand fast. Now, all Paulus could do was hope against hope that Manstein's troops would be able to break through.

Manstein's forces were led by General Hermann Hoth. Hoth and his Fourth Panzer Army drove through the sub-zero weather toward Stalingrad. By December 19, the rescue troops were within forty miles of their target. Two days later, they had only thirty miles to go before reaching Stalingrad.

Inside the city, the situation had become more and more desperate. Both the Russian and German troops were exhausted from the fighting. It had not let up for four long months. Countless German soldiers, wounded, starving, frostbitten—and desperate—chose to kill themselves.

Some of the wounded and many of the officers were airlifted out of the besieged city from the last open emergency air strip. But most of the troops were left to die in the trap that Stalingrad had become.

Then Manstein's rescue army got to within thirty miles of the city. Hoth sent a message to Paulus: "Hold on. We are coming." Spirits inside Stalingrad rose. Rescue was on the way! Hitler had not abandoned them, after all! They could hear the artillery outside the city. If they could hang on for only a little while longer, they would be rescued!

But it was not to be. As Hoth's troops began
the drive to cover the last thirty miles, the
Russians lashed back. Without warning, the
Fourth Panzer Army was faced with hard-
fighting Russian troops. And the Russians
were well equipped. They had warm winter
clothing and plenty of arms and ammunition.
The German rescue troops could not get past
the Russians. The harder they tried, the more
resistance the Russians put up. And Soviet
reinforcements continued to pour in.

Above: Russian troops in warm winter clothing. Below: Hope runs out for the poorly clothed German troops in Stalingrad.

In the middle of this rescue thrust, Manstein got news of an attack on his northern lines. The Russians were threatening his entire Army Group Don. Immediately, Manstein ordered Hoth to abandon his drive to Stalingrad. He must send one of his panzer groups north. He would have to do as well as possible with his remaining troops.

The drive to rescue the Sixth Army at Stalingrad had failed. Suddenly, the Nazis found themselves in mass retreat on all the Russian fronts. They simply were not strong enough to resist the determined Russians. Hitler could not defeat Russia.

The rescue troops pulled back on Christmas Eve, 1942. The German troops inside Stalingrad saw their hope shattered. This time, there would be no false hope of rescue. They truly had been abandoned.

The German troops spent the Christmas "holidays" in total despair. They knew now that they would be defeated. Thoughts of home and better days and lost dreams crushed their spirits.

One more mail plane would fly out of Stalingrad before the air strip was taken by the Russians. Many of the soldiers were given a chance to write one last letter home. In these letters, the Germans said their last goodbyes. They wrote of their love and concern for their families and friends. They wrote of their sadness at knowing they would never go home again. They wrote of these terrible last days in this city of rubble and blood. But even more strongly, they poured out their hopelessness, bitterness, fear, and anger at being left to die without hope.

The Nazis decided to read these letters before delivering them. They wanted proof for the civilians at home of the excellent morale of the "heroes" of Stalingrad. Instead, they were shocked at the overwhelming evidence of the desperately low morale of these doomed troops. Needless to say, the letters never reached their intended destinations.

Marshal Georgi T. Zhukov (above) set out to take defenses at Leningrad from orders of Premier Joseph Stalin (below).

January 8, 1943, was icy cold and windy. The German troops inside Stalingrad were startled to see a white flag. It had been raised at the Russian line at the edge of the city.

The Germans who saw it thought it might be a trick. But they held their fire. Three Russian officers walked slowly into the city. They looked very young. And they looked very warm in their winter uniforms.

The Russians gave the German officers a note for General Paulus. In the note, Russian General Rokossovsky wrote of the desperate situation of the German troops in the city. Though they had fought bravely and well, the note went on, their army was cut off. Any further resistance would be hopeless. If Paulus would surrender, the Russians would feed the German prisoners, provide them with warm clothing, and care for the sick and wounded. Rokossovsky gave Paulus twenty-four hours to reply to the demand for immediate surrender.

Having handed over the note, the three Russian officers walked out of Stalingrad to await General Paulus's answer.

Because Hitler had refused to permit Paulus to save the Sixth Army while it had still been possible, there were no longer any alternatives. Paulus knew that surrender was the only sensible course. He radioed Hitler. But he knew what Hitler's reaction would be to the word "surrender." So he asked instead for "freedom of action."

Paulus should not have radioed Hitler. Once more, Hitler absolutely refused to hear of a surrender. He had not permitted his Sixth Army to retreat when it might have saved them. And he was not about to let them give up to the Russian army now.

His decision led to the final destruction of an army that Nazi Germany would never be able to replace.

The Russians waited. When they had received no answer in twenty-four hours, they knew what had to be done. On the morning of January 10, 1943, the Russians aimed five thousand guns at Stalingrad.

The Russian bombardment of Stalingrad was so intense that more than 40,000 had been killed.

At the order to fire, the guns opened up. A barrage of bullets and shells descended on the city. For six days the Russian guns blasted away at the city and the Germans trapped inside. The Russian barrage also wiped out the German's emergency landing strip. The one last slim route of escape was destroyed.

Nothing faced the Germans now but certain death.

Suddenly the Russians ceased to fire. Once more, Russian officers gave General Paulus a chance to surrender. Once more, Paulus asked Hitler for freedom to act.

"We are out of ammunition," Paulus radioed Hitler. "We are out of food. We are out of medical supplies. Further defense is senseless. Collapse is inevitable."

These Red Army troops are ready to join the fighting in Stalingrad.

"Surrender is forbidden," Hitler replied. "Sixth Army will hold their position to the last man and the last round and by their heroic endurance will make an unforgettable contribution toward the establishment of a defensive front and the salvation of the Western world."

After Hitler's refusal, things happened quickly. By January 28, Paulus had practically no army left. The Russians had wiped it out.

On January 30, Paulus radioed another message to Hitler. "Final collapse cannot be delayed more than twenty-four hours."

That evening, Russian troops pushed their way into Paulus's headquarters in the basement of the Univermag Department Store. One last radio message went out from the trapped Germans. It read, "The Russians are at the door of our bunker. We are destroying our equipment."

When Adolf Hitler received the message, he launched into glowing praises of General Paulus and his Sixth Army. He promoted Paulus to Field Marshal. He also boosted the ranks of 117 other officers inside Stalingrad. His hope was that officers of such high rank would not surrender to the enemy.

The promotions and praise did no good. Paulus surrendered. What little fighting spirit was left in the Germans evaporated before noon on February 2.

That afternoon, a Russian plane approached Stalingrad. The pilot looked down on the city. Nothing could be seen but rubble, wreckage, and burning buildings. The pilot clicked on his radio. "No sign of fighting at Stalingrad," he reported.

That ended one of the saddest and most senseless sieges of World War II. That last message also signaled to the world that the Nazis could be defeated. This time they had been whipped because of Hitler's pride and stupidity.

Two months earlier, General Paulus had had 285,000 top fighting troops. He could have saved them. Because Hitler had not permitted his retreat, at the end of those two months only 91,000 German soldiers were left. They were taken prisoner by the Russians. Only 5,000 of them ever saw Germany again.

Above: Two German soldiers are marched out of a ruined building by their Russian captor. Below: The remnants of Paulus's Sixth Army were taken prisoner by the Russians and marched around the edge of the ruined city.

Stalingrad was a slaughterhouse for the Germans. This picture shows all that remained of the Nazi troops in a sector southwest of the city.

Stalingrad was a slaughterhouse for the Germans. And it was a turning point in the eventual defeat of Adolf Hitler and the government he called the Third Reich. The Nazis were run out of Russia, and Hitler lost his only chance to conquer the lands and treasures of that vast, rich country.

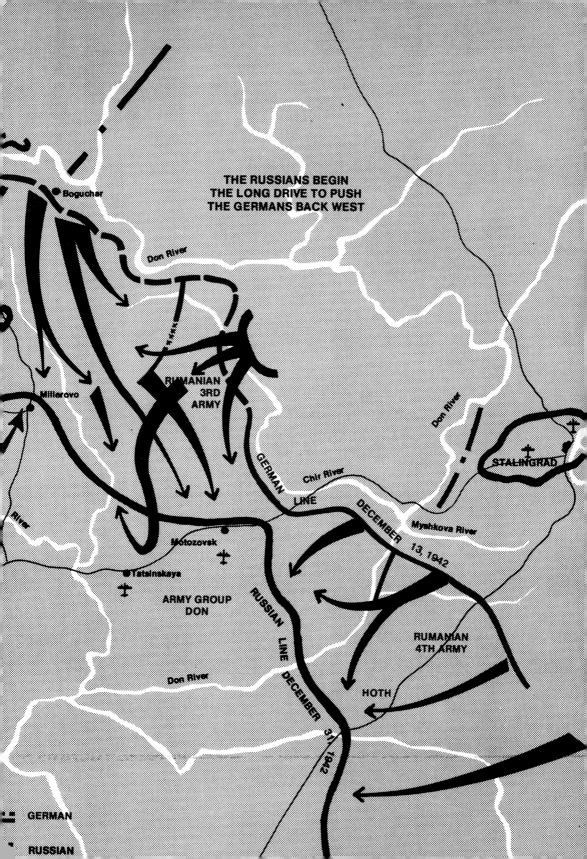

THE RUSSIANS BEGIN
THE LONG DRIVE TO PUSH
THE GERMANS BACK WEST

Boguchar

Don River

Millerovo

RUMANIAN
3RD
ARMY

River

Motozovsk

Tatsinskaya

ARMY GROUP
DON

Don River

Chir River

GERMAN
LINE

RUSSIAN
LINE
DECEMBER
31 1942

DECEMBER 13 1942

Myshkova River

STALINGRAD

Don River

RUMANIAN
4TH ARMY

HOTH

GERMAN

RUSSIAN

In the name of the people of the
United States of America,
I present this scroll to the
City of Stalingrad
to commemorate our admiration for
its gallant defenders whose courage,
fortitude, and devotion during the siege
of September 13, 1942 to January 31, 1943
will inspire forever the hearts of all
free people. Their glorious victory
stemmed the tide of invasion and
marked the turning point in the
war of the Allied Nations against
the forces of aggression.

May 17 1944

Franklin D Roosevelt

Washington, D.C.

INDEX

*Page numbers in boldface type
indicate illustrations*

About the Author

A native of Alabama, G.C. Skipper has traveled throughout the world, including Jamaica, Haiti, India, Argentina, the Bahamas, and Mexico. He has written several other children's books as well as an adult novel. Mr. Skipper has also published numerous articles in national magazines. He is now working on his second adult novel. Mr. Skipper and his family live in North Wales, Pennsylvania, a suburb of Philadelphia.